The Riddle of Destiny

Theme: **Destiny**

Heather Savini

Series Editor: Terence Copley

Biblos Series

RMEP

RELIGIOUS AND MORAL EDUCATION PRESS

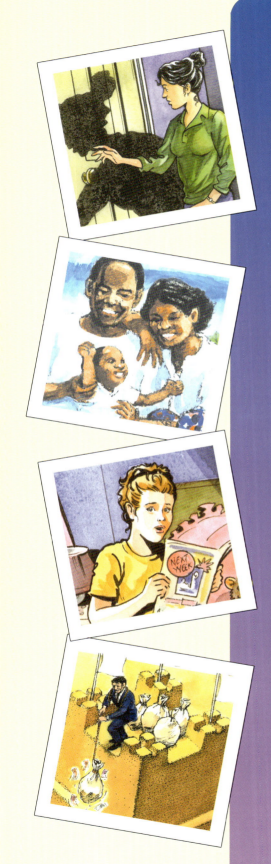

What this book is about

This book is about the destiny of the cosmos and the destiny of humankind. It looks at different answers to questions such as: Why are we here? Where are we heading? Does everything happen by chance? Does the cosmos have a design of which humans are a part and therefore a purpose which can be discovered? You will be introduced to narratives from the Bible about the purpose of creation and the part humans may play in this. You will also meet people from the Bible who discovered what they believed was their God-given destiny and a way of living which enabled them to arrive at their destination.

The Bible is a special collection of books which is taken seriously by Jews, Christians and Muslims. Some Jews and Christians would say that what makes the Bible special is that it records God's message for humankind. For people with no religious beliefs, it is still important as one of the most influential books so far in the history of the western world.

As you read this book, you will not be asked to believe (or to disbelieve) in God or in the religions which respect the Bible. But you will be asked to think about narratives from the Bible and to use the special clues provided to help you understand this collection of texts which goes back for more than 2500 years. Some clues are about context, how the narrative fits into the rest of the Bible. Others are clues to beliefs and customs that are like keys to unlock the narrative. You will also be asked to reflect on the beliefs and values of the people in these pages and to **reflect on your own beliefs and values**. At one time, many people thought that if something was in the Bible, it must be true. Some people assume the opposite now – if it's in the Bible, it must be *untrue*. We're asking you not to go along with what other people used to think or what they think now, but to **think for yourself**.

Although only a few extracts from the entire Bible appear here, every Bible narrative belongs to the Bible's complete narrative, in the way that any chapter belongs to the full book. The theme of the whole narrative is from Creation to Promise (Hebrew Bible/Christian Old Testament) or Creation to Re-creation (Christian Bible).

The Bible always deals with
- what people are like

  and
- taking God seriously.

What do *you* think people are like?

What do *you* take seriously?

What do *you* think taking God seriously might involve?

Contents

1. **Choosing Our Destiny:** 4
   The Tower of Babel (Genesis 11:1–9)

2. **Cosmic Destiny:** 9
   Creation from Its Beginning (Genesis 1–2)

3. **Cosmic Destiny:** 14
   The End and Re-creation (Revelation 21:1–22:5)

4. **Discovering Personal Destiny:** 19
   Gideon's Challenge (Judges 6:11–24)

5. **Discovering Personal Destiny:** 24
   Jesus' Mission (Luke 2:41–52)

6. **Living out God's Destiny for Humankind in the Kingdom of God** 28
   (Matthew 5:3–10)

In this book you will explore:

1. How the choices people make affect their destiny
2. How one person's destiny is linked to the destiny of others and the destiny of the cosmos
3. How some people accept God's involvement in their personal destiny
4. How some people who take God seriously seek to fulfil their destiny by living life as God intended it to be lived

UNIT 1

Choosing Our Destiny!

The Tower of Babel

In this unit you will explore:

1. How a person can influence their personal destiny by choosing either:
   - to live according to their own self-made plans;
   or (for the religious believer)
   - to co-operate with God's plans for their destiny.

2. A biblical narrative which demonstrates:
   - where self-made and self-centred plans can lead;
   - why humans are often at odds with each other.

This unit raises some important questions about the way people live their lives. Consider these questions before investigating what the narrative opposite has to say on the subject. Make a note of your own response and any different views others may have expressed, so that you can refer to these later. At the end of the unit you will have another opportunity to reflect on the differing responses to these questions.

Questions

1. What is the purpose of human life?
2. How far can people choose and influence their personal destinies?
3. What might be the consequences of people being self-centred?
4. Why do people often find it so difficult to work together?
5. Why might co-operating with each other enable people to achieve more worthwhile goals?
6. Why might belief in God encourage people to work better together?
7. Why might story-form be an effective means of getting across important truths about life?

'Glory to humans in the highest and confusion to people on earth!'

Ages ago, people everywhere were united by a common language. Also, they trusted what God had in mind for them. But when they gave up their nomadic life east of Canaan to settle down to a more sophisticated city life-style, on a plain in Babylonia, their priorities changed. Greater security meant they could now dispense with God and take care of their own destiny!

Increasing self-confidence and arrogance led to a desire to leave their lasting mark on the area. A city with a huge tower would impress everyone, and show just how powerful they were if their enemies tried to conquer them and expel them to the far corners of the earth.

However, pride in themselves and their construction skills with bricks and tar, were turning into a threat against God himself. As the tower rose towards God's heavenly territory, they dreamt of their fame when they would take over God's chief-executive role in the universe!

It was time for God to intervene before people's big-headedness got the better of them. God threw these highfliers into confusion by interfering with their communication system. Instead of speaking a common language they found themselves babbling in lots of different languages! Not surprisingly building came to an end, as they were unable to work together because no one could make sense of what any one else was saying! Frustrated and angry, they had to leave their unfinished city (which became known as Babel) and set off in different directions to seek alternative destinies. The different languages naturally spread with them.

For the time being, people would have to keep their feet firmly on the ground because their unity had been shattered through pride and it would take a long time before they could get back that co-operative spirit which enabled them to achieve great things together. Priorities needed to be sorted out. God's amazing plans for a glorious destiny for his creation were still waiting to be unfolded. People had to learn to work with God, rather than pursue their own self-centred agenda.

FREELY ADAPTED FROM GENESIS 11:1–9

Clues

On page 5, the writer has elaborated on the original, concise biblical narrative to incorporate some of the interpretation which biblical scholars give to this account. The final paragraph has also been added.

Read the Tower of Babel narrative in the Bible (Genesis 11:1–9). Then use these clues to help you understand what the biblical writer may be getting at. They will help you to answer the 'Reflection, Response' questions.

Do you think this is history or myth?

- This narrative does not appear literally to be history but describes symbolically the turbulent relationship between ambitious humankind and God. A symbolic story is called a 'myth'. It is not to be taken as literally true but contains truths about life.
- This is a very old narrative and God is described anthropomorphically (meaning 'in human terms') to convey his nearness to people.
- The Hebrews' knowledge of their physical universe was naturally limited. As life was sustained by the sun and rain from above, God was believed to be 'up there'. The sky was assumed to be the 'floor of heaven' and the ceiling of our world.
- The narrative is probably adapted from accounts of the origins of Babylonian ziggurats (temple-towers forming a gateway to heaven), whose ruins are still found in Iraq.
- Jews today have different views about this narrative; so do Christians. Some Jews and Christians take this narrative literally. Others regard it as myth.

What did the biblical writer believe about God and human destiny?

- Many religious believers, e.g. Jews, Christians and Muslims, believe that their personal destiny is linked to God's plan for the whole cosmos and therefore they should try to live according to God's agenda.
- In this narrative the Hebrew writer challenges the view that people are clever enough to do without God and set up their own agenda for living.
- The writer may have chosen the tower to represent rising human pride, which seeks to bring down and dismiss God.

Why are there so many languages?

- The Hebrews realized that different languages hindered people from working together and may have concluded that God had created languages to prevent people getting the better of him!
- God's intervention in this account is not necessarily punishment, but may be prevention, so that people can't selfishly misuse their power and skills.
- Myths (symbolic stories) were often used as a means of providing explanations to puzzling features of human life. Here an explanation is given for the variety of languages on Earth: God had brought them into being.

Why Babylon and Babel?

- 'A plain in Babylonia' refers to the region of Mesopotamia (modern Iraq) between the rivers Tigris and Euphrates. Babylon, dating from around 3000 B.C.E., was its chief city. It came to be used as an offensive term because it had such a corrupt and ungodly reputation. Hence, it is a good setting for a tower built as a monument to the fame of a people who ignored God's purposes and substituted their own goals.
- 'Babylon' means 'gate of God'. The writer plays on the words, combining Babylon with 'balal', meaning 'to mix or confuse', to form 'babel'. The English word 'babble' for incomprehensible sounds or speech derives from this.

Reflection, Response

Discuss

1. Why did the people in the story decide to build a tower?
2. What human characteristics might the tower represent?
3. In what other ways do you think the people might have used their skills?
4. Why do people sometimes make unwise decisions?
5. In what ways might people be trying to 'make a name for themselves' and 'leave a lasting mark' nowadays?
6. Why do some people lead self-centred lives?
7. What leads some people to choose to co-operate with what they believe are God's plans for their lives rather than their own agenda?
8. What causes some of the confusion and chaos in the world today?
9. What does it feel like to be unable to communicate verbally with someone?
10. What causes divisions in the human family today?

Reflection, Response

Record

1. Read the Tower of Babel narrative from the Bible (Genesis 11:1–9) and say what you think the Bible text is getting at and why. Identify the additions made to the original version by the writer of the adaptation 'Glory to humans in the highest and confusion to people on earth' and comment on them. Would you emphasize the same points as this writer does? Why? Why not?

2. 'A myth is true to life rather than literally true.' How might this statement apply to the Tower of Babel narrative?

3. Why might this narrative written about 2500 years ago still have relevance today? Use examples, e.g. the Twin Towers disaster in New York on 11th September 2001, to illustrate your reasons.

4. Record examples of 'Tower of Babelism Syndrome' that you notice in everyday life, e.g. examples of people's pride, self-centredness and over-ambitiousness. Note the consequences of this behaviour. (A photographic record might be produced with captions or a display tower of bricks with the examples recorded on each brick.)

5. Mime or combine with music and dance the Tower of Babel account to dramatize its message.

Find Out

1. Research the origins and purpose of ziggurats. (A web search will reveal photographs and information.) What do they tell us about the people's religious beliefs at that time?

2. Discover what you can about concerns that many languages are now becoming extinct. Is this desirable? Find out about Esperanto. (Discuss with your language teachers.) Is a common language a good idea? Think about possible choices: English, Chinese, Esperanto, ... Would we ever agree? Give your reasons.

3. Investigate what types of human projects (e.g. buildings, scientific discoveries, inventions) have a lasting effect, for good or bad, on society.

4. Find evidence to illustrate how far human beings are really free to make their own choices and decisions in life, e.g. in friendships, clothes, careers, leisure activities and health. What other factors limit personal free will, e.g. personal aptitude, character, disease, advertising?

5. Draw up a brief questionnaire for religious believers in school or the local community to explore:
   - what they believe about the purpose of human life
   - what they believe about God's plans for their personal destiny and the destiny of the cosmos
   - what difference this makes to their personal choices and decisions in everyday life and their long-term destiny.

Imagine

1. What difference would it make if only one language was spoken on Earth?

2. The Faith Communities in the United Kingdom made a Millennium Commitment:

> 'To work together for the common good,
> uniting to build a better society,
> grounded in values and ideals we share:
>
> > community,
> > personal integrity,
> > a sense of right and wrong,
> > learning, wisdom and love of truth,
> > care and compassion,
> > justice and peace.
> > respect for one another,
> > for the earth and its creatures.'

If these values and ideals were put into practice by people living in your neighbourhood, what changes to restore the human family do you think might be seen? Examples might be: no fear of walking in the streets, no vandalism, more educational opportunities for all ages.

Questions

Look again at the questions at the beginning of the unit (page 4). Have you changed your initial response? Why? Why not?

Concepts

Here are some concepts you have encountered in this unit:
- the purpose of human life
- free-will
- self-centredness
- the break-up of the human family.

UNIT 2

Cosmic Destiny

Creation from Its Beginning

In this unit you will explore:

1. How the cosmos came into being and has evolved.
2. Some religious perspectives on why the cosmos exists.
3. The options of:
   • belief in a chance destiny
   • belief in God's planned destiny.

This unit raises some important questions about human beings and the cosmos. Consider these questions before investigating what the narrative on the next page has to say on the subject. Make a note of your own response and any different views others may have expressed, so that you can refer to these later. At the end of the unit you will have another opportunity to reflect on the differing responses to these questions.

Questions

1. Is our cosmos purposeless?

2. Is our cosmos the result of random chance?

3. Is our cosmos God's planned creation to fulfil God's purposes?

4. Are human beings the result of chance factors?

5. Are human beings part of God's plan for the whole universe?

6. Are science and religion contradictory or complementary?

7. Can there be any type of truth in a story that is not literally true? (Think of Aesop's fables.)

The cosmic clock starts ticking ...

How did creation happen?
A scientist might tell this story.

In a flash, out of nowhere, a tiny fireball of cosmic embryo ignited. Thirteen billion years later its force still pulsates throughout the cosmos and drives it towards its destiny, fuelled by its primordial energy. Time, space and everything there is came into being with this rather small bang!

Boiling gas was released, catapulting everywhere. Clouds of cooling gas whirled, expanded and puffed ever onwards. About half a billion years after it all began, the pull of gravity caused them to collide and give birth to billions of galaxies of stars.

More than 4 billion years ago, in the Milky Way galaxy, a cloud of dust and gas shrank, spinning faster into a disc shape. Its core became hotter and denser until it flashed into life, giving birth to a star – the Sun. In the surrounding disc nine planets began to form, including Earth, generated by light and energy from the Sun's nuclear fusion reactions. The cosmic egg had hatched.

A precise combination of raw material (dust and mud) from the surface of Earth, with energy and heat, took over 4500 million years to evolve intelligent life – human beings!

The cosmos is special because the finely balanced forces of nature produced conditions that were just right for life to evolve. But a different cosmic story could have unfolded. It is even possible that many diverse universes exist!

Meanwhile our universe continues to expand at 100 000 miles per second ...

Consider these questions:

1. What is your reaction to such an amazing story?
2. Do you wonder exactly where you are and why you are here?
3. If, as the text says, you are made from stardust, who are you and do you really matter?

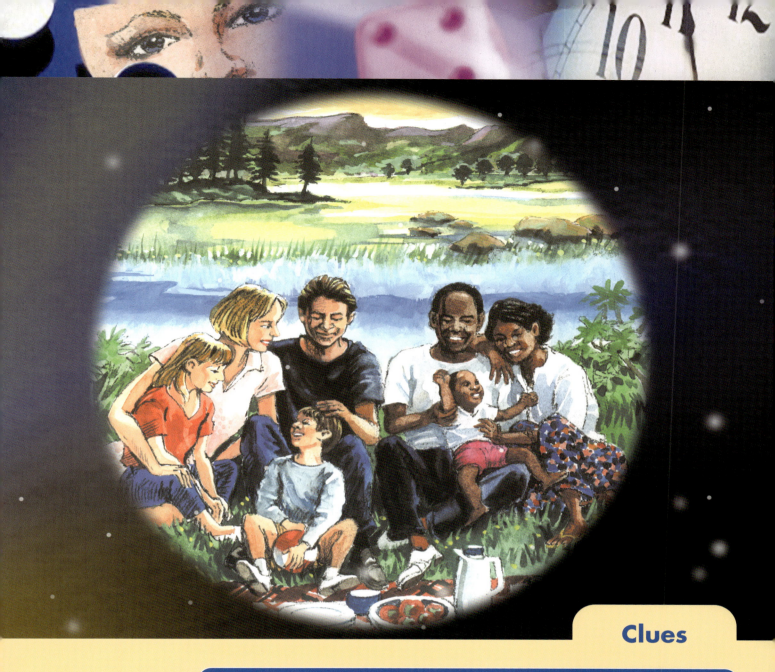

Clues

Read these two clues.

The scientific narrative

Scientists generally accept that:
- The Big Bang could have produced a vast number of possible outcomes. The probability of evolution of an earth like ours is small but not entirely a matter of random chance.
- Alternatively, our cosmos and the laws of physics operating in it could be the result of random chance.

Religious truth

Religion uses stories to convey important religious truths which otherwise are difficult to express and grasp. These symbolic stories are known as 'myths'. Literal truth has a different function from religious truth. The former states the facts of the matter and the latter draws out the meaning.

Now read Genesis 1:1–2:4a and Genesis 2:4b–25. These are two Jewish religious narratives explaining beliefs about why the cosmos was created.

Clues

Use these clues to help you understand the Bible narratives and see what the writers may be getting at. They will help you to answer the 'Reflection, Response' questions.

Jewish creation narratives

- All ancient civilizations produced their own versions of the world's origins and significance. Obviously they had limited scientific knowledge about the universe but these narratives emphasized religious truth.

- The Jews have two different creation narratives incorporating their own distinctive beliefs about God and the destiny of God's creation. These narratives were not intended to be mainly scientific accounts of how the cosmos originated (they actually contradict each other in their details) but rather they state why the universe was created – as a deliberate act of God who had a purpose and a plan for it.

- Although the narratives are different, they both proclaim:
  – that God, not chance, is responsible for creation
  – that creation is overwhelmingly good
  – that humans have a special relationship with God and a special part to play in accomplishing God's plan for them and the cosmos.

- The older narrative, in Genesis 2:4b–25, tells about Adam and Eve in the Garden of Eden. It focuses on the forming of man and woman as God's first act of creation, with the rest of creation directly serving humankind's needs. The close relationship between God and people is emphasized.

- The narrative in Genesis 1:1–2:4a, written later, describes creation in a six-day time-scale. It is a more sophisticated account, where God is more remote and orders creation to happen. There is an emphasis here on the importance of the Sabbath (Friday sunset to Saturday sunset), with God resting on the seventh day after completing his work. Human beings are made in God's 'image'. This identifies them as God's representatives, created to share the responsibilities of creation.

Different responses to these Jewish narratives

Biblical material is interpreted differently within both Judaism and Christianity, depending on whether believers have a traditional or more modern approach to their Scriptures.

- Some Jews and Christians believe creation took place exactly as recounted in these two narratives and they reject alternative scientific accounts of creation.

- Other Jews and Christians believe that both the scientific and the biblical versions help their understanding of creation, the former explaining *how* creation might have come about and the latter *why* it might have happened.

- Atheists, who reject belief in God, deny any truth in the biblical creation narrative, believing that only the scientific accounts have anything to say about creation.

Reflection, Response

Discuss

1. What evidence might have led the writers of the Jewish creation narratives to believe God was responsible for creation?
2. What evidence would have convinced them that creation was good?
3. What might have led them to believe they were partners with God in fulfilling the destiny of creation?
4. In practice, what might such a partnership require from people?
5. How do you account for people's different interpretations of biblical material, e.g. literal and more liberal?
6. Why are religion and science often seen as enemies?
7. What are your own feelings and questions as you learn more about the complexities and vastness of the universe?

Record

1. From the two biblical narratives about creation choose quotations which express the religious truth claims in the accounts. Devise an interesting way of presenting these quotations and their truth claims on paper.
2. Write a conversation between:
   (a) A religious person who believes the universe was created by God literally as the Genesis accounts state.
   (b) A religious person who believes the universe evolves in the way it does because God designed it to develop in that way.
   (c) An atheist who believes that chance factors, not God, resulted in evolution taking the particular course it has.

   Include reasons for the points made. (Work in threes, each taking a role. Think about which role is hardest to get into and why.)
3. Write a fictitious story which conveys an important message you would like to pass on to readers.

Find Out

1. Research the latest scientific knowledge on the origins of the universe. If possible use the internet. Keep a personal or class record of developments over a period of weeks by checking websites. Write a personal or class report on your findings and comment on: (a) the significance of these for humankind; (b) why this scientific progress might be interesting and relevant to some religious believers and not to others.
2. Record an interview with a person who believes that their life is part of God's plan and with one who believes that chance is in control and get both to explain how their beliefs influence the way they live. Use these interviews as the basis for a class discussion or more formal debate with prepared speeches. You could use some of the information gathered in Unit 1, 'Find Out' question 5.
3. Collect articles from the media about people who you believe demonstrate a sense of purpose in their lives. Categorize them to identify motivations, e.g. personal ambitions, political ideology, desire to improve the planet, commitment to religious belief. Write a statement that draws on your evidence to demonstrate the significance of purpose in people's lives.
4. Identify examples from contemporary songwriters who describe the problems of life and the search for personal destiny and meaning. Create a design or poster to focus on your findings.

Imagine

1. Imagine you had the opportunity to design a cosmos and life-forms within it. Consider such questions as: Would the cosmos be vast and mysterious? Would life-forms be programmed or left to their own devices? Would there be time? Identify either in a diagram or in note form:
   - the key features of your blueprint
   - how your world would develop
   - your hopes for your world.
2. Imagine the instructions God might give to the parents of a new-born baby about its purpose and destiny. Design a handbook to be delivered with the baby!
3. Imagine you were in control of the existing universe, with complete power to change and run it. What would your major delights and worries be? What changes would you make in the first week?

Questions

Look again at the questions at the beginning of the unit (page 9). Have you changed your initial response? Why? Why not?

Concepts

Here are some concepts you have encountered in this unit:
- creation explained in non-conflicting religious and scientific terms
- story as the conveyor of religious truth
- cosmic and personal destiny as dependent on chance or on divine design.

UNIT 3

Cosmic Destiny

The End and Re-creation

In this unit you will explore:

1. A Christian perspective on the final destination of humankind and the cosmos.
2. What some scientists think will happen ultimately to our cosmos.
3. The significance of the belief that God is in control, for the everyday life of the religious believer.
4. The continuing struggle between good and evil in our world.
5. Human fears and hopes for the future, of both religious believers and non-believers.

This unit raises some important questions about the future of the cosmos. Consider these questions before investigating what the narrative opposite has to say on the subject. Make a note of your own response and any different views others may have expressed, so that you can refer to these later. At the end of the unit you will have another opportunity to reflect on the differing responses to these questions.

Questions

1. Must everything that begins have an ending? What about human beings and the human race?
2. If God exists, how far can humankind understand God's plan and timetable for the cosmos?
3. How important is the conviction that evil cannot have the last word, however much it appears to be getting away with it?
4. What difference does it make if you believe there is a 'happy' ending rather than a disastrous one for the cosmos?

A Christian's 'view' of
the end of the cosmos

'How *is* it all going to end?' we often ask when things go wrong. Let me tell you about my time in prison. I'm not a criminal, but the Government did not like my views and pledged to stamp out the group that I belonged to. Some of my friends had actually lost their lives through terrible torture. I was depressed. It seemed as if the authorities would win. They had the power. All I had to hold on to was my belief that the new way of life was worthwhile.

Is it so revolutionary to try to live your life in a better way? Is it wrong to stand up against the rottenness and wrong around us and ask for a better deal for the weak in society? Is justice to be ignored? Are people to be exploited by dictators? Are people to be taken for a ride by their leaders? We wanted people to have a better deal because our leader had shown us what we were really destined for: a worthwhile life of service to God, putting others before ourselves. (Only in that way can God's great plan for creation be accomplished and its perfect destiny be achieved.) We should have known that it could all end in disaster, because our leader had lost his life in trying to promote this radical approach to living.

So I was feeling very pessimistic in my island prison, when I had the most incredible experience! I wrote it down almost as it happened, so I could share it with you. I would describe it as a vision, a sort of science-fiction film, a waking dream, about the end of everything! Sometimes it was terrifying. At other times it was peaceful. It gave me back my courage because it showed me in picture language that everything was going to be all right – that God was in control, that God would deal with evil and restore creation to the perfection designed for it at the beginning of time. I also realized I did have a part to play in helping this grand finale come about.

So close your eyes and try to 'see' what I saw. I wrote this some time ago, so I hope the language won't appear too old-fashioned or the pictures too strange. See what you can make of it!

Listen to:

Revelation 21	vv. 1–8 – The New Heaven and Earth
	vv. 9–14 – The New Jerusalem
	vv. 18–21 – The Foundation Stones
	vv. 22–27 – Light and Life
Revelation 22	vv. 1–5 – The Tree of Life

Clues

Use these clues to help you understand the Bible narrative and see what the writer may be getting at. They will help you to answer the 'Reflection, Response' questions.

Who wrote this passage and why?

▸ John, the author of the Book of Revelation, was probably a Jewish Christian who received his visions during a period of imprisonment, when Christians faced terrible persecution.

▸ The Roman Emperor Domitian, who ruled 81–96 C.E., proclaimed himself Lord and God and persecuted those refusing to worship him. This political situation was such a crisis for Christians that John 'saw' a cosmic battle between evil and God. The battle ends in victory and peace for those who remain faithful to Christ.

The Book of Revelation

▸ Revelation is a challenging book, full of visions containing symbolism which is strange to the modern reader. It is typical of a type of writing common both before and after Jesus' time, known as apocalyptic ('apokalyptein' in Greek means 'to uncover' or 'to reveal') or 'revelation' writing.

▸ Such literature appeared in times of crisis and was often pessimistic, stressing evil's power, and concentrating on how everything would come to a dramatic end.

▸ In contrast, this book of Revelation is positive and emphasizes the final victory of Christ in the New Jerusalem. It highlights the Christian belief that God was in control at the beginning of creation and will be in control at the end for re-creation.

The meaning of the vision

▶ The visions are not literal statements giving a map and timetable of what is actually going to happen at the end. But they do present pictures that give Christian imaginations reassurance that ultimately all will be well.

▶ In this symbolic vision good transforms evil to complete God's plan for creation's destiny. Creation is recreated and the new Jerusalem is holy and perfect. John's vision reveals that:

  – the present heaven and earth are replaced (21:1)
  – the sea, feared because it symbolized chaos and evil, disappears (21:1)
  – the New Jerusalem has a heavenly origin (21:2) and design (21:10–21)
  – God is now present with his people and the covenant finally fulfilled between them (21:3).
  – no temple is required because Christ has given direct access to God, so temple sacrifices are no longer necessary (21:22)
  – holiness and light pervade the city (21:23)
  – all nations come together to show the city's universal nature (21:24 and 22:2)
  – no evil can enter the city (21:27).

The number 12

▶ The number 12 and its multiples symbolize wholeness. The 12 foundation gems refer back to the 12 gems on the breastplate worn by the High Priest in the old Jerusalem Temple. They stand for the 12 tribes of Israel, especially responsible for carrying out God's purposes. In 21:14 the 12 gems are linked to the 12 apostles of Jesus, pointing to God's renewed people.

▶ Later, Jews and Christians developed this symbolism by attaching gems to months of the year. This is the origin of birth stones for birth months.

Eschatology

This is the term used for the examination of beliefs about the time and nature of the final stage of cosmic history. 'Eschatos' in Greek means 'last'.

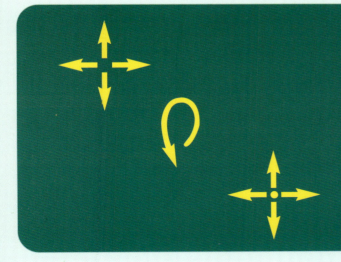

What scientists predict

Physicists today believe that the gradual expansion of the universe since it exploded billions of years ago is slowing down. In the future, the universe may:

▶ go on expanding for ever

▶ stop expanding and shrink as gravity pulls everything back to a point of infinite density that takes up no space, just as it was in the beginning

▶ collapse to where it started from and have another Big Bang, generating a new universe, possibly very different from this one.

Reflection, Response

Discuss

1. What difference will God's presence in the New Jerusalem make to the people? See 21:4–8.
2. What do you understand by God's declaration, 'I am the first (Alpha) and the last (Omega), the beginning and the end' in 21:6?
3. Why do you suppose precious stones and metal are used to describe the New Jerusalem?
4. Recall the many references to the number 12 and its multiples. Why is it used so frequently?
5. The 'glory of God' shines on the city (21:23). What do you understand this to mean?
6. Why do you think John felt so hopeful after his fantastic vision?
7. Which images appeal to you from John's vision? Explain why.
8. What signs would religious believers today see to support their belief in God's eternal union with creation?
9. Why do you think part of the vision is often read at Christian funeral services?
10. How do you react to the scientists' views of how the cosmos will end?
11. How might these views tie in with cosmic re-creation presented by John in Revelation?
12. Science-fiction writers often focus on eschatological (end-of-time) events. What feelings about the future can these produce?
13. How may belief in God help people approach the future?
14. How important might our individual contribution be in influencing the destiny of the cosmos?

Record

Either …

Produce a class basket of 'fruits' from the tree of life which you would like children to enjoy as a positive beginning to the new millennium, e.g. enthusiasm, opportunities, pleasure from learning. State how these fruits might be seen as contributing to God's destiny for our world.

Or …

Select and colour 12 precious stones to form a symbolic design and include (in separate writing or incorporated into your design) what you want each one to stand for and why, in your vision of the ideal, perfect city, e.g. fairness, honesty, safety. Describe how your design compares with John's New Jerusalem by looking at the similarities and differences.

Or …

The tree of life produces leaves which are intended for 'the healing of the nations'. Draw these leaves and say in words or incorporate in your design what sort of healing those leaves will provide to restore the world to a more wholesome state, e.g. peace for the warring, food for the hungry, fairness for the oppressed. Write about the causes of the wounds which hurt the nations of the world.

Find Out

1. Ask a science teacher to explain in more detail the latest scientific views on the end awaiting the cosmos. What feelings do these provoke in you?
2. What evidence exists that people have 'visions' nowadays?
3. Research the religious symbolism of the precious stones mentioned and the religious significance of birth stones.
4. Organize a class debate on 'This house believes good is stronger than evil' to discover people's views.

Imagine

1. Select six negative experiences from your everyday life and transform them into positive ones! (For example, make up with a friend who has let you down; own up to the real reason why your homework was not done; give up a bad habit.) What was needed to make the change? (Forgiveness, courage, hard work, etc.) If people made more effort to move from the negative to the positive, how might the world be transformed?
2. Imagine you are coming to the end of your life. What would you be proud of having contributed to the good in the world and what would you wish could be erased from your life's record?
3. Think of the positive achievements of the human race in the last century which might demonstrate that we are progressing towards a better way of living (e.g. technology to provide more food, increased communications). Where might religious believers see God working alongside people in guiding world progress?

Questions

Look again at the questions at the beginning of the unit (page 14). Have you changed your initial response? Why? Why not?

Concepts

Here are some concepts you have encountered in this unit:
- beginnings and endings
- apocalyptic writing (writing that 'reveals' things) about the end of time
- Christian beliefs about the 'last things' or eschatology
- the religious belief in the triumph of good over evil: God over chance
- the religious belief in the perfect, eternal union of God with creation.

UNIT 4

Discovering Personal Destiny

Gideon's Challenge

In this unit, through the example of Gideon, one of Israel's leaders, you will explore:

1. How some people feel 'called' by God to take on a particular role.
2. How such people, inspired by God, find the strength to fulfil this destiny.
3. How one person's destiny affects the destinies of other people.
4. Why it is that the individuals God calls to undertake difficult tasks may seem surprising choices.

This unit raises some important questions about the way people live their lives. We shall learn about one person in the past but we shall also ask, what can be learnt from them for the present or future? Consider these questions before investigating what the narrative on the next page has to say on the subject. Make a note of your own response and any different views others may have expressed, so that you can refer to these later. At the end of the unit you will have another opportunity to reflect on the differing responses to these questions.

Questions

1. Why might some people feel 'called' or compelled to do a particular task or job?
2. Why might some people be willing to entrust their destiny to such a 'call'?
3. Why do you think God is seen as working through people's weaknesses in some Bible narratives?
4. What influence can a person's example have in shaping the destinies of others?
5. What evidence is there to suggest that it might be God who inspires people to achieve great things?
6. In what ways do people believe that God communicates directly with them nowadays?

From Cowardice to Courage!

I was a nobody. As the youngest in a family from a minor tribe, I never seemed to live up to anyone's expectations. But through a strange encounter my life changed. I became someone with a special destiny! I was threshing wheat in my father's winepress, hidden away to avoid the Midianites, who stole our precious crops. Out of the blue appeared not a Midianite, but an angel from God! Was I seeing and hearing things?

'The Lord is with you, brave and mighty man!' Who was he greeting? Thinking he was having me on, I answered back that if God really was with us, why didn't he save us from the Midianites, just as he had delivered our ancestors from the Egyptians? But I had put my foot right in it because I was immediately ordered to save my people from the Midianites myself! How ridiculous! Then came the crunch line:
'I myself am sending you.'

Now, there was no mistaking God's command. But who was I to take on this task? He insisted that I would be successful. 'You can do it because I will help you.' What an offer! What words of power! Suddenly I felt I *could* do it. But I still needed more reassurance that it wasn't a hoax. So I plucked up the courage he said I had, and asked for proof of his identity. When I set out meat, bread and broth on a rock under the oak tree to welcome him, an amazing sight followed. The visitor's stick made the food go up in flames like a burnt offering to God and he disappeared. I was terrified that I might drop dead because I had actually seen God's angel's face, but – thank God! – I was assured

I would survive. Immediately I made an altar with a pile of stones, naming it 'The Lord is Peace' to mark the special place where I had come face to face with God's angel and put my destiny in God's hands.

In spite of my fears, I did get rid of those scavenging Midianites as well as the foreign gods. I am even remembered as one of the twelve judges who helped Israel to settle in Canaan, the land God had promised us. My people, the Israelites, had so much to learn about trusting God and not being disloyal. It was difficult to believe that God could make Israel's history and his planned destiny for all creation coincide.

Certainly, only God could have had enough faith in me to make a somebody from such a nobody! You see what happens when you let God's spirit shape your destiny!

FREELY ADAPTED FROM JUDGES 6:11–24

Clues

Use these clues to help you understand the Bible narrative and see what the writer may be getting at. They provide information on the background to this story and will help you to answer the 'Reflection, Response' questions.

Canaan and the Midianites

- In about the twelfth century B.C.E. the Israelites, having escaped from slavery in Egypt, settled in their 'promised land' of Canaan (later called Israel, then Palestine and now known by some as Israel and by some as Palestine). This proved to be a very difficult time for the Israelites, not least because they were tempted to worship the Canaanite gods such as Baal, the male fertility god, and his female partner, Asherah.

- The Midianites were descendants of Abraham's son Midian, who had been sent to live in the deserts of Syria and Arabia. They were nomads, using camels to travel through the desert, and they became enemies of the Israelites because they harassed the farming Israelites for their crops. This is the earliest record of the use of camels in war.

Clues

Leaders in times of crisis

- The Hebrew Bible/Christian Old Testament implies that whenever the Israelites forgot their part of the covenant or agreement with God to live as God wanted them to, they were overwhelmed by their problems. In these crises a leader, inspired by God, would rally them together to face up to their enemies and to remind them to be faithful to the God of their ancestors and not the Canaanite god, Baal. There were 12 of these leaders, called 'Judges' because of their leadership and good judgement.

- Gideon is the fifth Judge listed. He is challenged by God to help his people and he responds with total dependence on God's support, getting rid of their Baal worship (Judges 6:25–32) and overcoming the Midianite enemy (Judges 6:33–7:25, 8:4–21).

- The Israelites wanted to make Gideon their king because he accomplished so much for them, but he reminded them that God was their king. But, later, the last Judge, Samuel, reluctantly appointed Israel's first king, Saul.

Religious symbols

- Oak trees were considered sacred in Israel.
- Religious law required a bread offering to God to be without yeast because leaven (from the rising yeast in the bread) was a symbol of corruption. The burning up of the offering showed that God had accepted it.
- The altar's name, 'The Lord is peace', honours the God who promises peace to those who obey him. 'Peace be with you' ('shalom' in Hebrew) was the everyday greeting.

Theophany – an appearance of God

- 'Theophany' means the appearance of God to people. In the Hebrew Bible/Christian Old Testament, God appeared to chosen people, often in isolated places, near trees and on mountains. Shrines and temples were built to revere the place of God's presence.

- The ancient Hebrews had no problem about what form God took to appear on Earth. As humans were believed to be made in God's image, it seemed natural that if God appeared the form might be that of a human body.

- In very old Hebrew literature God dealt directly with human beings. As time passed, God was understood to be more distant and so needed messengers to communicate with people. These were in human form and often described as an 'angel of the Lord'. They had the authority of God because God had sent them.

- The Hebrew Bible/Christian Old Testament implies that God's appearances gradually ceased as the prophets came to be seen as the channel for God to reveal his will, although angels continued to make appearances from time to time.

Reflection, Response

Discuss

1. Why do you think Gideon had so little self-esteem?
2. What changed his view of his abilities?
3. How might this encounter have changed Gideon's understanding of God?
4. How might religious people explain God's choice of Gideon for this difficult task?
5. Why is courage considered an important quality? Can it be used for bad acts as well as good?
6. How can people become more courageous?
7. Do people still believe they are called by God to take on demanding roles?
8. Why do some people feel obliged to go along with what they understand as God's requests?
9. If God is real, why aren't problems sorted out directly by God rather than through relying on people?
10. Do people who take God seriously believe God still makes appearances? If so, how might God be recognized?

Record

1. Write Gideon's diary entry after he had received this 'call' from God. Include in your extract:
   - why he is so surprised to have been chosen by God for this tough assignment
   - what his fears are in carrying out his new mission
   - how he feels about having to forget his own plans for the future
   - how he plans to make a success of his assignment
   - what he thinks of God's way of doing things.
2. Write the conversation between Gideon's parents and brothers when they hear about Gideon's encounter. Include a variety of reactions to the unexpected event and challenge.

Find Out

1. Research the work of 'The Gideons' organization. (If possible use the internet.) Why do you think this name was chosen for this organization? Was it a good choice?
2. Discover the effects of Desmond Tutu's inspired leadership in:
   - challenging racism in South Africa, when Archbishop of Johannesburg
   - chairing the Truth and Reconciliation Committee.
3. Cut out reports of people's courage from newspapers and magazines and make a 'Wall of Courage' display. What might be the sources of these acts of courage (e.g. inner or external factors)?
4. Discover which careers in the past were often described as 'vocations' and why. Your careers adviser may help you. How has the meaning of the word 'vocation' changed in its more recent use, when some school subjects are described as 'vocational'?

Imagine

1. Imagine a modern assignment that God might want someone to tackle. Describe the assignment and the type of agent God might pick to accomplish this task. Give details of the support God might offer the candidate.
2. Imagine a personal destiny which you would like to fulfil but for which you lack the courage. What steps could you take to find that courage?

Questions

Look again at the questions at the beginning of the unit (page 19). Have you changed your initial response? Why? Why not?

Concepts

Here are some concepts you have encountered in this unit:
- vocation
- weakness transformed into power
- inspired leadership
- theophany (appearance of God).

UNIT 5

Discovering Personal Destiny

Jesus' Mission

In this unit you will explore:

1. How the 12-year-old Jesus pursued his personal destiny.
2. How his life and death would affect the world's destiny.
3. How his example inspired a modern young man searching for his destiny.
4. The sacrifices people may be called to make in fulfilling their destinies.

> This unit raises some important questions about the way people live their lives. We shall learn about an incident in the past but we shall also ask, what can be learnt from this for the present or future? Consider these questions before investigating what the narrative opposite has to say on the subject. Make a note of your own response and any different views others may have expressed, so that you can refer to these later. At the end of the unit you will have another opportunity to reflect on the differing responses to these questions.

Questions

1. Are some children naturally more 'religious' or 'spiritual' than others? Why might this be so?
2. What influences a child's religious understanding and development?
3. What factors might have influenced Jesus in discovering his own destiny?
4. Was he free to make his own decisions or was he programmed by God?
5. Why might people who respond to God's call often have to suffer?
6. What impact did Jesus' life and death have on the destiny of the world?
7. How does Jesus' example influence the destinies of people today?

The Jerusalem Journal
'King of the Jews' crucified!

Jewish leaders jeered, saying, 'He saved others; let him save himself if he is the Messiah whom God has chosen.'

He died after crying out, 'Father! Into your hands I place my spirit.'

Our reporter found this article, published about 18 years ago, which had predicted that Jesus would hit the headlines again.

Did Jesus fulfil his destiny?

Missing Boy Found!

Distraught parents, Joseph and Mary, from Nazareth in Galilee have been reunited with their missing son after three days of searching. As usual, this time 12-year-old Jesus was able to join them. With the festival over, the party had set off for Nazareth with their group of pilgrims.

In his Father's house!

After travelling for a whole day Joseph and Mary realized that Jesus was not with their friends and relatives as they had assumed. Frantic, they rushed back to Jerusalem. It was only on the third day of looking that they discovered him in the Temple listening to the teachers as well as questioning them. People in the crowd said how impressed they were by Jesus' intelligent contributions! Normally his mother might have been proud of her son's ability but an eye-witness reports that she seemed very hurt when she asked him why he had done this to his father and her. Not surprisingly, she added that they had been terribly anxious about his disappearance. What did surprise our onlooker was the boy's reply: 'Why did you have to look for me? Didn't you know that I would be in my Father's house?' Jesus' parents seemed puzzled too, but it was not the right moment for further discussion. They were just so relieved and happy to be reunited.

From Nazareth ...

Our reporter in Nazareth has been trying to find out more about this young man since there seems to be something special and purposeful about him.

One of Jesus' friends says:
'I reckon Jesus got carried away by the chance to quiz the experts and lost his sense of time, not wanting this unique opportunity in the Temple to end! His mother usually keeps a close eye on him. Perhaps she was testing how responsible he is as a "son of the law" after his Bar Mitzvah ceremony.'

Jesus' rabbi at the Nazareth synagogue says:
'I don't condone Jesus' behaviour in worrying his parents, but he is a good lad with an amazing understanding of the Jewish religion. I often find it difficult to answer Jesus' tough questions! He would have been in his element learning more about God from our holy teachers. Certainly, Jesus is developing a close relationship with God through his knowledge of our Scriptures and prayer. He wants to discover God's purpose for his life. It's a privilege to have such a pupil!'

Jesus' mother says:
'I admit my son's behaviour seems out of character. Although Jesus is officially an adult Joseph has to keep an eye on him and between the two of us we let him down by not checking he was heading homewards. Jesus' explanation of his behaviour was so sincere that I realize it is another piece to fit into the puzzle of his destiny. But all that matters for the moment is that he is safe. Who knows, perhaps he'll become a teacher? I can't see him settling for the building trade like his dad!'

Our reporter comments that he doesn't think this is the last we shall hear about Jesus. He predicts he'll make headlines again.

Now read:

the original narrative in Luke 2:41–52.

Luke 23 records the trial, crucifixion, death and burial of Jesus. You can read this to discover what destiny awaited Jesus.

25

Clues

Use these clues to help you understand the Bible narrative and see what the writer may be getting at. They will help you to answer the 'Reflection, Response' questions.

The journey to and from Jerusalem

- This incident is the only glimpse given in the New Testament of Jesus' boyhood.
- At puberty a Jewish boy becomes officially a 'son of the law' or Bar Mitzvah, and is received as an adult member of the Jewish community, taking responsibility for himself concerning the demands of the Torah. As an adult, Jesus would now be eligible to attend the Passover Festival in Jerusalem, which was 70 miles from Nazareth.
- Passover is the chief Jewish religious festival, commemorating the Exodus from Egypt (Exodus 12:1–27; Deuteronomy 16:1–8) when the Hebrews were spared from death by the angel of death passing over their houses in the last plague. Lasting seven days, in Jesus' time it had to be held in Jerusalem.
- It appears strange that Jesus' parents travelled for a whole day before missing him. But as it was the custom for the women to set off home earlier, Mary might have assumed that Jesus was with Joseph and vice versa. Alternatively, after a boy's Bar Mitzvah the father had oversight of the son and it has been suggested that perhaps Joseph forgot this!

The Temple – 'My Father's House'

- For Jews, the Temple was the place where God's presence could be especially felt. Today only the Western Wall remains of the second Temple built on this site.
- During Passover the Sanhedrin (Jewish Supreme Court) met publicly in the Temple to discuss religious issues. Jewish rabbis and priests also sat in the Temple courts, teaching and discussing.
- Jesus' description of the Temple (v. 49) implies that the Jewish belief in God being like a father had become an intimate personal experience for him.
- Christians later came to believe that Jesus as 'son of God' had a unique and special relationship with God which influenced his own personal destiny as well as that of the whole world.

Jesus as Messiah

- Jews at this time desperately hoped for the arrival of God's Messiah in order to get rid of Roman rule and set up God's kingdom on earth. 'Messiah' in Hebrew (or 'Christ' in Greek) means 'anointed one'. Anointing with oil symbolized the coming of God's spirit on to a person at their appointment to a particular task.
- 'Jesus' means 'the Lord saves' in Hebrew. Jesus 'the Christ' was believed by his followers to be appointed by God as Saviour from sin and evil.
- Sons usually followed in their father's trade, which for Jesus meant some kind of building work. Matthew 13:55 asks about Jesus, 'Isn't he the carpenter's son?', while Mark 6:3 has 'Isn't he the carpenter, the son of Mary …?' But note that the Greek word 'tekton' (often translated as 'carpenter') means a worker in stone, wood or metal.

Reflection, Response

Discuss

1. How true to life does Jesus' family appear in this episode?
2. How would you describe Jesus' personality from this incident?
3. Could Jesus have refused to co-operate with God's plans for him? Why?/Why not?
4. What sacrifices were involved in Jesus' decision to work with God?
5. As a boy Jesus was very interested in God and was keen to engage in religious discussion. Why might young people nowadays not take belief in God very seriously?
6. How do role models influence young people in shaping their destinies?

Record

1. The following references in the Bible record special moments in Jesus' life and demonstrate how his personal destiny unfolded. Draw his lifeline and plot in these decisive events. The extracts could be divided between the class to read and recount the key points to the others.

Luke 2:8–20	Luke 9:18–20	Luke 23:13–25
Luke 2:41–52	Luke 9:28–36	Luke 23:26–43
Luke 3:21–22	Luke 19:28–40	Luke 23:44–8
Luke 4:1–13	Luke 22: 14–23	Luke 24:1–12
Luke 6:12–16	Luke 22:39–46	Luke 24: 36–43
Luke 6:17–19	Luke 22:47–53	Luke 24:50–53

2. Not everyone is called to meet such difficult challenges as those of Gideon (see Unit 4) and Jesus. However, young people do have to face up to a variety of challenges, such as influences, opportunities, decisions and commitments, as they prepare for adulthood. Write about some of these challenges, saying whether you consider them daunting or to be welcomed and why. How might they relate to your personal destiny?

3. Compose a poem or story which conveys the nature and importance of sacrifice in human life. You will need to:
   - reflect on the different types of sacrifices people are prepared to make, e.g. donating a kidney; endangering their own life to rescue someone else; limiting spending on themselves to benefit others.
   - analyse what turns an action into a sacrifice and what makes people willing to make such sacrifices.

Find Out

1. How do Jews and Muslims regard the life and death of Jesus? Interview some Jews and Muslims and refer to textbooks and, if possible, the internet.

2. Who are the people nowadays who set examples for others to follow in living their lives? Assess the qualities they possess as role models.

3. Research the story of Tim Goggs, a young Christian killed by a landmine while rescuing a colleague, when working for the Halo Trust in Afghanistan. (If possible use the internet.)
   - What influences contributed to Tim's sense of purpose and achievements?
   - How would you describe Tim's personal destiny?
   - In what ways was Tim following Jesus' example?

Imagine

1. You are a television interviewer planning to interview Jesus: this can be either the 12-year-old Jesus (after the episode in Jerusalem) or later in his life (when he had begun his ministry). What questions would you choose to put to him? (For example: Why have you so much faith in God? Why are your family unhappy about what you do? Why do you feel compelled to 'work' for God?) How might Jesus respond to your questions?

2. Write a letter to the parents of a young person who has had to face danger in fulfilment of their destiny, telling them what you think of their son's/daughter's decisions and achievements. This might be to Tim Goggs' parents or someone else, real or imaginary.

Questions
Look again at the questions at the beginning of the unit (page 24). Have you changed your initial response? Why? Why not?

Concepts
Here are some concepts you have encountered in this unit:
- Messiah/Christ
- free will
- sacrifice
- personal example.

UNIT 6

Living out God's Destiny for Humankind in the Kingdom of God

In this unit you will explore:

1. Jesus' revolutionary teaching regarding the destiny of humankind in terms of 'The Kingdom of God'.
2. A sample of this challenging teaching known as the Beatitudes (Matthew 5:3–10).

This unit raises some important questions about the way people live their lives. Consider these questions before investigating what the narrative opposite has to say on the subject. Make a note of your own response and any different views others may have expressed, so that you can refer to these later. At the end of the unit you will have another opportunity to reflect on the differing responses to these questions.

Questions

1. According to Jesus, how does God expect people to live their lives and co-operate with God's destiny for people?
2. Why do people live so differently from the way God wants them to live?
3. Why do many people never seem to be truly happy?
4. What can bring people real fulfilment and happiness?

Living in God's Way

The Beatitudes

'Beatitude' comes from the Latin word 'beatitudo', meaning 'blessing'. 'Blessed' in the original Greek means 'free from worry and joyful'.

This well-known biblical passage introduces a collection of Jesus' teaching known as The Sermon on the Mount (Matthew 5:1–7:27 and Luke 6:20–49). It illustrates Jesus' understanding of a new way of living. If humankind is to fulfil its true destiny according to God's plans then this new way of living is essential.

God blesses those who acknowledge they need to rely on God, because they are citizens of God's kingdom.

God blesses those who are distressed by suffering and need, because they will be comforted by God.

God blesses those who do not seek to be important, because God's promises are for them.

God blesses those whose aim is to live in God's way, because God will meet their needs.

God blesses those who forgive others, because God will forgive them.

God blesses those whose motives are pure, because they will experience God's presence.

God blesses those who build peaceful relationships, because they belong to the family of God.

God blesses those who are despised for living in God's way, because they are citizens of God's kingdom.

Freely adapted from Matthew 5:3–10

Clues

> Use these clues to help you understand the Bible narrative and see what the writer may be getting at. They will help you to answer the 'Reflection, Response' questions.

Jewish background to the kingdom of God

- The Hebrews (later called the Israelites and then the Jews) originally accepted that God was their king, so they had no need of an earthly king. But later, they demanded an earthly king in order to copy other nations.
- The Jews were often defeated in battle and found themselves ruled by other nations. They saw this as punishment from God for their disloyalty to him. They longed for the time when God would intervene directly to rescue them from their enemies, especially at the time of Jesus, when they were ruled by the Romans.
- The Jews came to believe that God's special agent, whom they called the 'Messiah', meaning 'the anointed one', would appear and restore them to world leadership and establish God's kingdom.

Jesus' understanding of the kingdom of God

- Jesus seems to have identified himself with the Messiah but rather than proclaim this publicly, he left people to work it out for themselves from his words and actions.
- Jesus announced that God was breaking into the human realm and God's kingdom was being established. (It would be finalized in the future.) But God's message was not what the Jews had expected. Instead of defeating the Romans, God was challenging the power of evil because that was what really spoiled human well-being. This meant that people needed to reassess and transform their way of life as God's priorities were very different from human values. It was qualities such as love and service, not power and wealth, which would transform the world and enable people to realize their true destiny as citizens of God's kingdom.
- 'The kingdom of God' was Jesus' main topic of teaching and has been described as 'a kind of logo' for Jesus. This was not a physical place but the reign of God in people's hearts and lives. Jesus challenged people to a new way of living which would enable them to fulfil the destiny God had planned for them, as citizens of the kingdom. The parables, as well as many of Jesus' short statements and the collection of teaching known as 'The Sermon on the Mount' (containing the Beatitudes), present Jesus' teaching on different aspects of God's kingdom.
- In the Beatitudes, Jesus identifies a list of people who are blessed by God because of their contribution to God's way of living as citizens of his kingdom. This list highlights the difference between human priorities and those required by God if a person is to live according to God's way.
- By living a life of love and service to others, Jesus demonstrated that true citizens of God's kingdom place God's will at the centre of their lives rather than their own self-interest.
- The kingdom of God is sometimes referred to as the kingdom of heaven because Jews avoided pronouncing God's name out of reverence.

Reflection, Response

Discuss

1. Who might people normally consider blessed (i.e. happy and fortunate)?
2. Do people find real contentment from material wealth, ambition, power and popularity? Why?/Why not?
3. What do the Beatitudes identify as the characteristics of worthy citizens of God's kingdom?
4. What is your reaction to the list of people blessed by God in the Beatitudes? Are they the sort of people you would expect to see on such a list? Why?/Why not?
5. What sort of contentment might the people blessed in the Beatitudes experience?
6. Why is there such a difference between what God values in people and what humans value?
7. How might a person's destiny change if service to other people became a top priority?
8. What makes some people rely on God to help them live their lives, while others prefer to rely on themselves?
9. Why are people today sometimes despised for 'living in God's way'?

Record

1. Write down the aspects of God's destiny for humankind listed in the Beatitudes, e.g. reliance on God, forgiveness and peaceful relations. Explain why these might be regarded as revolutionary and 'topsy turvy'. How might they improve the quality of people's destinies? How difficult might they be to achieve in practice?
2. Write a story about a real or an imaginary person who might be considered to be a citizen of God's kingdom (select one of the categories mentioned in the Beatitudes, e.g. those who suffer, forgive or work for peace). Tell their story – what they have done and the effect it has had on others. Explain why you think this person would be granted citizenship of God's kingdom.
3. Compare what it might mean to live as a citizen of God's kingdom and to live as a worthy citizen of your country. Identify any similarities and explain key differences. (Consider, for example, the aim of each type of citizenship and the qualities and behaviour required of each type of citizen.)
4. Compose a poem to the people who you consider deserve to be blessed in life, following the pattern of the Bible's 'Beatitudes'.
5. Design a crest or symbolic picture for Jesus' 'Kingdom of God' based on the concepts in the Beatitudes and explain the significance of your design.

Find Out

1. Lord Longford said he would like to be remembered as 'an outcaste of outcastes'. Research how he tried to live out his Christian destiny as a citizen of God's kingdom. (If possible use the internet.)
2. Research the work of both Baroness Caroline Cox and Sue Ryder as peace-makers in war zones. (If possible use the internet.)
3. Identify events, movements or personalities that for Christians might be glimpses of the presence of God's kingdom in our world. Produce a collage or classroom frieze entitled 'Kingdom Come!' containing this evidence.
4. Interview people and find out what their recipes are for discovering happiness and fulfilment in life. Analyse and comment on your findings in an article for a young people's magazine. (Select people from different backgrounds and ages. Draw up questions to ask them: e.g. What do you understand 'happiness' and 'fulfilment' to mean? How can a person identify them? What contributes to 'happiness' and 'fulfilment' in life? Is 'happiness' permanent? How might 'fulfilment' be achieved?)

Imagine

1. The kingdom of God has been described as 'an invitation to a vision of how things should be'. Imagine your vision of how life should be and compose a manifesto which presents your ideas in words or design.
2. Imagine how the concepts of 'destiny' and 'the kingdom of God' could be expressed through dance, music, poetry, story or drama. Present one or more ideas either in note form, orally or as performance, e.g. assembly.
3. Continue Archbishop Carey's parody on the Beatitudes, which symbolizes our topsy-turvy values today:

   > Blessed are the famous, for they will enjoy the praise of men.
   > Blessed are those who are rich, because they will inherit the earth.
   > Blessed are the mighty, because they will become more powerful yet …

Questions
Look again at the questions at the beginning of the unit (page 28). Have you changed your initial response? Why? Why not?

Concepts
Here are some concepts you have encountered in this unit:
- revolutionary teaching
- blessedness/happiness
- kingdom of God/heaven.

Closing questions to consider

What is the destiny of humankind?
How does God fit in:
(a) for non-believers; (b) for believers?

Religious and Moral Education Press
A division of SCM-Canterbury Press Ltd
A wholly owned subsidiary of Hymns Ancient & Modern Ltd
St Mary's Works, St Mary's Plain
Norwich, Norfolk NR3 3BH

Copyright © 2003 Heather Savini

Heather Savini has asserted her right under the Copyright, Designs and Patents Act, 1988, to be identified as Author of this Work.

All rights reserved. No part of this publication may be reproduced, stored in a retrieval system, or transmitted, in any form or by any means, electronic, electrostatic, magnetic tape, mechanical, photocopying, recording or otherwise, without permission in writing from the publishers.

First published 2003

ISBN 1 85175 285 4

Designed and typeset by
TOPICS – The Creative Partnership, Exeter

Illustrations by Jim Eldridge • David Johnson • Neil Rogers

Printed in Great Britain by Brightsea Press for SCM-Canterbury Press Ltd, Norwich